RAILWAYS
of the
NORTH YORK MOORS

Compiled by
MICHAEL BLAKEMORE

GREAT NORTHERN

In the same series:
RAILWAYS OF THE YORKSHIRE DALES

Great Northern Books
PO Box 213, Ilkley, LS29 9WS

This edition 2005
First published by Atlantic Publishers 2001

ISBN 1 905080 04 2

© Michael Blakemore, 2005

Design and layout: BARNABUS DESIGN & REPRO, TRURO

Printed by THE AMADEUS PRESS LTD., BRADFORD

British Cataloguing in Publication Data
A catalogue for this book is available from the British Library

CONTENTS

The changing face of the North York Moors. Goathland station on 30th November 1965, almost nine months after closure under the ravages of the Beeching Plan. Wintry conditions on local roads were so bad that a diesel unit made an emergency run to carry schoolchildren to Whitby. Today Goathland is the centre of "Heartbeat Country" and a key source of traffic on the flourishing North Yorkshire Moors Railway. (John Tindale)

⚓ INTRODUCTION ⚓

Inviting a Lancastrian to write about the railways of the North York Moors might be considered to be akin to asking a football supporter to write about a rival team! Not so in this case! Many youthful holidays in Scarborough fostered a lifetime appreciation of the rocky coastline and the rolling moorland sweeping away from the sea.

It is a beautiful part of England and through and around it a tightly-linked little network of railway lines was built up which, interestingly, spanned almost the whole era of railway construction. Today the preserved North Yorkshire Moors Railway is one of our most famous 'heritage' lines but how many of the many thousands who come to visit it each year appreciate that it is also one of our most historic? In the first formative years of railways no less a person than George Stephenson engineered a route from Whitby to Pickering; but when it opened in 1836 it was a world away from what we see today. Horses plodded valiantly along it through Newton Dale and it took the arrival of the York & North Midland Company's railway from York to Scarborough in 1845 to inspire the conversion of the Whitby & Pickering into a 'modern' locomotive-worked line which eventually carried through coaches from London.

The last link in the network was not completed until nearly 50 years later when the Scarborough—Whitby line was opened in 1885, perhaps a logical connection between these neighbouring resorts and ports but a physically difficult one to achieve. Its arrival on the map was only a few years after two other latecomers — the boldly-engineered Whitby, Redcar & Middlesbrough Union line and the peacefully-rural Forge Valley branch.

The scenic delights of the railways of the North York Moors soon came to give pleasure to the many who visited and holidayed in the area, as well as giving service to local communities where they opened up travel opportunities, facilitated the carrying of goods and often provided a lifeline in harsh winters. However, it should not be forgotten that despite the apparently rural nature of the area, there were pockets of industry which the railways served; most notably, ironstone was mined in the Esk Valley and up in the wilds of Rosedale. These latter workings were reached by a mineral railway in a setting which could hardly be a greater contrast to the Ryedale branch in a largely agricultural district on the south west fringe of our area where the North York Moors start to soar away from the Vale of York.

Sadly, scenic railways in lightly-populated countryside do not make good economics and closures began as early as 1931 on the Gilling—Malton branch and continued during the 1950s. The 'Beeching Report' of 1963 foretold their total demise but they did not go without a fight; the closures of the Whitby—Pickering—Malton line south of Grosmont and the Scarborough—Whitby route were two of the most bitterly-contested cases of that whole unhappy period.

What remains today? The Esk Valley service between Whitby and Middlesbrough clings on to a tenuous life, while the North Yorkshire Moors Railway, operating between Grosmont and Pickering, is firmly established as a tourist attraction *par excellence,* its popularity further boosted by film and television appearances. Elsewhere, trackbeds have vanished beneath road improvements and building developments or have been taken back into the farmland from which they were once won. On the coast the trackbed of much of the Scarborough to Whitby route is a footpath and the scenery can still be enjoyed, albeit not from the comfort of a train.

This book does not set out to be a definitive history of any of the lines it features; all have been covered elsewhere in much greater detail and by more expert authors. It does, however, hope to give a flavour of a series of inter-connecting but highly-individual branch lines — some still much loved, others less well recalled — in the days before a changing world brought about their decline and fall.

In preparing this book, my thanks are due to all those photographers who recorded the railways of the North York Moors, in particular to Robin Lidster, Patrick Howat, David Sutcliffe, John Spencer Gilks, John Edgington and the Ken Hoole Study Centre at the Darlington North Road Station Museum for generously making pictures from their collections available.

MICHAEL BLAKEMORE

THE WHITBY & PICKERING RAILWAY

One of the area's most popular tourist attractions is the North Yorkshire Moors Railway, with thousands every year enjoying a steam-hauled journey through the superb scenery of Newton Dale and Fylingdales Moor. Few, however, probably realise what an historic railway it is.

The Whitby & Pickering Railway obtained its Act of Parliament in 1833, just three years after the Liverpool & Manchester Railway had begun the passenger railway system, but this was to be a very different type of operation. The WPR was to be a horse-powered railway and no less a personality than George Stephenson was engaged to engineer a route "for the employment of animal power". A natural route existed along the River Esk and through the glacial gorge of Newton Dale; a short tunnel was required at Grosmont but the originally-envisaged route called for a long tunnel between there and Goathland. However, this was abandoned in favour of a rope-worked incline at Beckhole on an average gradient of 1 in 15.

On 26th May 1836 the railway was opened throughout; the old port of Whitby was re-invigorated and passenger traffic exceeded expectations. Yet in less than a decade the railway revolution had left the WPR isolated. By 1839 the York & North Midland Railway, under the charismatic chairmanship of George Hudson, the so-called 'Railway King', had established its presence in York and in 1845 opened its line to Scarborough. Hudson, who had ambitions of becoming MP for Whitby, courted the WPR and promised the development of the town as a holiday resort. The Scarborough line brought with it a branch from Rillington (just east of Malton) to Pickering to meet the WPR and with its acquisition of the latter in 1845, the YNMR set about refurbishing it for locomotive haulage. Heavier rails were laid, the track doubled, its severest curves eliminated by deviations, stronger bridges built and new stations constructed. A new tunnel was also bored at Grosmont, the original being only wide enough for horse haulage.

Locomotives worked into Whitby for the first time on 1st July 1847 — but it was still not a through journey for the rope incline at Beckhole remained. It was an unsatisfactory situation which, spurred by some unfortunate accidents, drove the North Eastern Railway (as successor to the YNMR from 1854) to build a 4½-mile deviation line from south of Grosmont to join the original course near Fen Bog. This was opened on 1st July 1865, with a new station at Goathland.

By Edwardian times tourism was flourishing, only to be set back by the onset of war in 1914. In fact, during the war four miles of track between Pickering and Levisham were sacrificed, by singling the route, so that it could be used in support of the war effort and that section of the line remained single track until closure nearly 50 years later.

Traffic reached its peak between the wars. The LNER's famous 'Scarborough Flier' from King's Cross included through coaches for Whitby, while scenic excursions were run from the West Riding or Hull travelling out via Pickering to Whitby and returning over the coast line via Robin Hood's Bay (or vice versa).

Little changed during the 1950s under BR other than the appearance of diesel multiple units on many of the local services. However, publication in 1963 of *The Reshaping of British Railways* — the so-called 'Beeching Plan' — revealed that closure was proposed of all the rail links to Whitby. The result was one of the most fiercely-contested closure battles in the country, with local authorities disputing BR's claim that the Pickering line was losing £50,000 a year and pointing out the social need fulfilled by the railway in the winter months when villages such as Goathland were frequently cut off by road in severe weather.

It was all to no avail; the harsh reality of too many empty seats mid-week and mid-winter could not keep the economists at bay and the line between Rillington Junction and Grosmont was closed on 8th March 1965. The section from Grosmont to Whitby remained open, as the Esk Valley branch service to Middlesbrough had been reprieved to abate the furore created by the prospect of leaving Whitby rail-less. Interestingly, the Grosmont—Goathland section was re-opened on one occasion the following winter to carry schoolchildren into Whitby when the roads were blocked by snow — demonstrating that the protestors had made a valid point during the closure debate! However, the cost was charged to the North Riding County Council which found it prohibitive and the exercise was not repeated.

There, as with most closed branch lines, the story might well have ended. An attempt by local councils to re-open the route with the aid of subsidies collapsed but led to the formation of the North Yorkshire Moors Railway Preservation Society in 1967. Much hard work was to follow but on 1st May

1973 the line returned to life when the Duchess of Kent performed the public re-opening ceremony. Since then, the North Yorkshire Moors Railway has gone from strength to strength, becoming one of the country's premier preserved lines. The attraction of the superb National Park scenery, steam trains and delightful moorland villages like Goathland has brought visitors from all over the world, while the railway's association with the popular *Heartbeat* television series and, most recently, the Harry Potter film has placed it before huge new audiences. Its success seems set to continue.

Early days on the Whitby & Pickering Railway — a horse-drawn carriage approaches one of the timber bridges over the River Esk. (From The Scenery of the Whitby & Pickering Railway, *published in 1836 and illustrated by George Dodgson).*

Pickering station, looking north, on 25th September 1949. It was built to the design of G.T. Andrews of York, architect of the York & North Midland Railway. Unfortunately the fine overall roof was removed in 1952.

BR Class 3 2-6-2T No.82029 enters Pickering station with a train from Whitby in 1962. The destination would be Malton but for those whose horizons stretched wider the poster on the far platform recommends Thomas Cook's! The photograph shows the canopy which replaced the original roof; the lighting was not modernised, though, and gas lamps remain. (W.R. Mitchell)

An NER G5 0-4-4T finds a way through the woods of Newton Dale.

Winter in the Vale of Levisham — viewed from the warmth of the train LNER B1 4-6-0 No.61276 heads the 4.00pm Malton—Whitby round the curves on 20th February 1964.

One of the most attractive stations was Sleights, on the banks of the Esk. The level crossing has been replaced by a road bridge but traffic would have been very modest at the time of this view c1910. Note that the siding to the goods yard has a separate gate and also a short trap siding, occupied by a platelayers' bogie, to prevent wagons running on to the main line. (NRM 474/86)

J23 0-6-0 No.2453 leads a mixed goods on to the single track section south of Levisham in 1935. This class of strong 0-6-0s was introduced by the Hull & Barnsley Railway in 1889 but with the decline of the coal export trade in the late 1920s many were redeployed by the LNER to depots in the north east where they could be of more use. Malton, Pickering, Whitby and Scarborough sheds all had examples, the last two being withdrawn from Whitby in 1938.

The G5 0-4-4Ts introduced by the North Eastern Railway in 1898 put in some sterling service on the Whitby—Pickering route, their modest size belying their capacity to cope with the arduous duties involved. No.394 is seen departing from Levisham in 1935 with a train from Whitby which includes a horse box at the front.

LEFT: *The homely station of Goathland sees BR Class 4 2-6-4T No.80118 arriving with a Whitby-bound service in; a couple strolls up to the station just in time to catch the train. The tidy state of the station area is worthy of comment and is typical of times when rural stations were staffed with people to care for them. Water columns are provided at both platforms to replenish locomotives thirsty from long pulls from Pickering or Whitby; that on the end of the north platform has an elevated drainage bowl to prevent water running over the crossing.* (David Sutcliffe)

RIGHT, TOP: *Levisham has the charm of a remote yet well-tended wayside station, with no sign of the eponymous village from its platforms. This 1961 view is looking towards Pickering.* (David Sutcliffe)

RIGHT, BOTTOM: *Goathland station looking north in 1961. At the end of the station the gradient commences falling at 1 in 49. In recent years the preserved NYMR had added a footbridge and the station has featured as Aidensfield in the* Heartbeat *television series and in the* Harry Potter *film.* (David Sutcliffe)

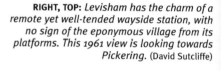

LEFT: *The new route constructed in 1865 to avoid the Beckhole incline was not without severe gradients of its own and climbed at 1 in 49 from Grosmont to Goathland. Here is G5 0-4-4T No.1316 manfully toiling up the last stretch of the bank into Goathland station.* (J.W. Armstrong Trust)

Grosmont station c1910. The two platforms of the Pickering line are straight ahead while the Esk Valley branch, served by a single platform, curves off to the right. An ironworks used to exist at Grosmont, occupying a site off to the right beyond the Esk Valley line. The signal box was closed by BR in 1972 when the line was singled to Sleights. (NRM 865/86)

A spectacular view from Larpool of the Whitby & Pickering line's approach to Whitby along the banks of the River Esk. On the left, descending to join it at Bog Hall Junction, is the WRMU line from Whitby West Cliff. In the middle distance the railway passes between the locomotive shed (on the left) and the goods depot (on the right) before curving round towards the terminus, later known as Whitby Town. The old port spreads about both river banks and is dominated by the ruins of Whitby Abbey.
(G.W. Wilson collection/Aberdeen University Library)

ABOVE: *LNER A8 4-6-2T No.69861 (rebuilt from a NER 4-4-4T in 1935) passes Beckhole with a Whitby—Malton train in 1956; the leading vehicle is a NER brake composite.* (J.M. Jarvis/Colour-Rail BRE160)

RIGHT: *K1 2-6-0 No.2005, in LNER apple green livery though not actually buil until after nationalisation, slogs up the bank into Goathland station, in Apr 1983. This locomotive, restored by the North Eastern Locomotive Preservatio Group, has been a regular performer on the NYMR.* (T.J. Edgingto

Whitby Town station dates from the rebuilding of the line in 1847 and G.T. Andrews was again the architect. By the time of this photograph on 3rd September 1978 only the Esk Valley service remained but the station was still staffed and offered 'Rail Express Parcels' facilities. Today trains are even fewer, the station unstaffed, facilities withdrawn and the buildings converted to commercial units. (T.J. Edgington)

Whitby locomotive depot in 1934. In the yard are two locomotives of NER origin, LNER F8 2-4-2T No.1581 and A6 4-6-2T No.693. The F8s were introduced in 1886 for suburban and branch line work; they were not the best-known of Whitby power in the Whitby area, but a number did work local services from Whitby and Malton sheds. The A6 is of greater interest as these engines were built as 4-6-0Ts in 1907/8 specifically to cope with the gradients of the Scarborough— Whitby line. Known as 'Whitby Willies', their power made them very welcome on this difficult route but their coal and water capacity proved inadequate so between 1914 and 1917 all were rebuilt with larger tanks and trailing wheels to allow larger bunkers. As 4-6-2Ts they became LNER Class A6 and remained on the coast line until displaced by even stronger locomotives in the late 1930s. (T.E. Rounthwaite)

THE RYEDALE BRANCH

Running through Ryedale, on the southern fringe of the North York Moors, was a rural branch line which led a charmed existence. In 1853 the York, Newcastle & Berwick Railway's Thirsk & Malton branch opened, bringing rail transport into this undeveloped agricultural district. Commencing actually at Pilmoor, on the main line south of Thirsk, it pursued a course between the Hambleton and Howardian Hills through Coxwold, Gilling and Hovingham to meet the Malton & Driffield Railway. The promoters of these two lines had visions of a through route from the North East to the Humber but that was by no means the most ambitious idea on offer in Ryedale.

In 1854 the Thirsk—Malton—Driffield route became a part of the new North Eastern Railway's growing empire and it was to this increasingly-powerful body that a local company, the Ryedale Railway, made an approach in 1862 to contribute to the building of a branch from Hovingham to Helmsley and Kirkbymoorside. The NER declined. However, another proposal was being floated in the area in the guise of the Leeds, North Yorkshire & Durham Railway. This envisaged a route from Leeds via Wetherby, Helmsley and Bilsdale towards the Cleveland Hills on the way to Stockton; more than this, it proposed branches to Scarborough and into Farndale. In the background lurked the presence in all this of the London & North Western Railway which was keen to achieve access into Teesside and whilst it seemed a fantastic scheme, it attracted favourable reaction in the area and the NER took such potential infiltration seriously enough to oppose and defeat it in Parliament. It also proposed a line of its own.

In 1866 the NER's own Gilling and Pickering Act was passed in Parliament; this branch would leave the T&M line at Gilling, head north to Helmsley then east through Kirkbymoorside to join the Whitby line at Pickering. Two years later the NER was seeking to persuade landowners to abandon the route between Helmsley and Pickering but pressure was exerted on the company to fulfil its commitments. Eventually the line was completed and opened in sections: from Gilling to Helmsley on 9th October 1871, on to Kirbymoorside (the railways omitted the second 'k' in spelling the station name!) on 1st January 1874 and ultimately to Pickering on 1st April 1875.

For the next 75 years the branch quietly served the villages and market towns of Ryedale until the more convenient service offered by buses brought its closure. The last trains ran between the main line junction at Pilmoor and Pickering on 31st January 1953, with the section between Kirbymoorside and Pickering being abandoned completely.

Remarkably, though, the rest of the Ryedale branch enjoyed another decade of life providing a goods service and seeing some quite colourful days when passenger trains returned. From 1932 summer Saturday trains between Scotland or the North East and Scarborough were routed off the East Coast Main Line at Pilmoor and down through Gilling to Malton. This was to enable them to avoid congestion at York station where they would have to reverse on the busiest days of the year. It was not, however, a straightforward operation as a double reversal was required at Malton — at Scarborough Road Junction to reverse onto the link onto the main Scarborough line, then again in the station before proceeding coastwards. These services were resumed after the war and continued until the last trains of the 1962 season. The motive power was sometimes rather exotic and LNER Pacifics were occasionally recorded treading carefully along this byway.

On 19th March 1963 a parcels train was derailed at Sessay Wood Junction, Pilmoor, and in order to get traffic moving again quickly the pointwork was replaced by plain track. It was soon decided not to reinstate the junction and with the abandonment of the section between there and Husthwaite Gate the summer holiday excitement came to an end.

Passenger trains in the form of ramblers' excursions (which had long been popular) continued to visit the Ryedale stations, including those on the Gilling—Malton line which had become an early closure victim in January 1931. Another source of passenger traffic was Ampleforth College for which trains were run to and from Gilling at the beginning and end of terms. Outward excursions also originated on the Ryedale branch to destinations such as Llandudno and Largs and a programme of Sunday School specials to Scarborough formed the very last passenger workings on 27th July 1964.

Such a rustic anachronism could not survive the relentless cuts of the mid-1960s and the local goods — by then only thrice weekly — ran for the last time on 7th August 1964.

ABOVE: *LNER D49/2 4-4-0 No.269 The Cleveland runs into Kirbymoorside with a Pickering—York local over the Ryedale branch in August 1937; the signalman stands ready to exchange single line tokens.* (Colour-Rail NE18)

RIGHT: *Some of the most interesting trains over the Ryedale line were the summer Saturday trains between Scotland or the north east and Scarborough which travelled from Pilmoor via Gilling and Malton. A V2 2-6-2 is seen passing Ampleforth station with a train for Scarborough in the summer of 1961.* (David Sutcliffe)

LEFT: *After closure Nunnington station was converted to a cafe with the platform, fenced off along the edge, making an ideal terrace. On 26th May 1960 the crew of J39 0-6-0 No.64928 took advantage of it to enjoy a break while working the branch goods.* (Alan Lillywhite)

BELOW: *A summer Saturday Newcastle—Scarborough service threads through the cutting at Thormanby Hill, between Pilmoor and Husthwaite, behind LNER B1 4-6-0 No.1274 on 30th July 1949.* (J.W. Hague/D.V. Beeken collection)

Curtains for the Ryedale branch on 7th August 1964. J27 0-6-0 No.65894 is seen in the yard at Coxwold while working the final goods train to Gilling. (C.A. Allenby)

The small station at Slingsby had generous goods facilities including a three-storey grain warehouse. In 1961 it still had the services of a porter-signalman who is pictured exchanging single line tokens with the fireman of B1 4-6-0 No.61216 on a Scarborough train. (David Sutcliffe)

Coxwold in NER days presents a modeller's delight. A train from Pickering is in the westbound platform while the signals are off for a train from the Pilmoor direction to cross it in the station. (P. Howat collection)

Ten years after the end of passenger traffic, Gilling station still looks busy and well-kept — but this is August 1964 and there is not long to go. Porter-signalman Gilbert Hugill is on the platform as a BR 204hp 0-6-0 diesel shunter deals with a coal wagon and brake van on the pick-up goods. This view is looking west towards Coxwold. The layout through Gilling station is unusual as the Malton line (left) and Kirbymoorside line (right) come in as two separate single tracks. (Patrick Howat)

A splendid setting at Hovingham around 1900, after 'Spa' had been added in 1896 to the station name in a bid to promote tourist traffic. Some locals have joined the station staff in front of some interesting items just delivered or ready for despatch — a cartwheel and an axle, but where was the other wheel?! (P. Howat collection)

ABOVE: *The summer Saturday trains to the east coast and the specials for Ampleforth College sometimes brought locomotives as big as Pacifics into Ryedale. These ran to Gilling with the Pacific which had brought the train up from King's Cross working through from the East Coast Main Line junction at Pilmoor. When this connection was severed, the trains ran to Malton where the London engine was detached at Scarborough Road Junction and another engine coupled on to the other end to continue to Gilling. Here is prestige power in the distinctive shape of A4 No.60017* Silver Fox *at Scarborough Road on 30th April 1963 bringing scholars back after the Easter holiday.* (Ken Hoole)

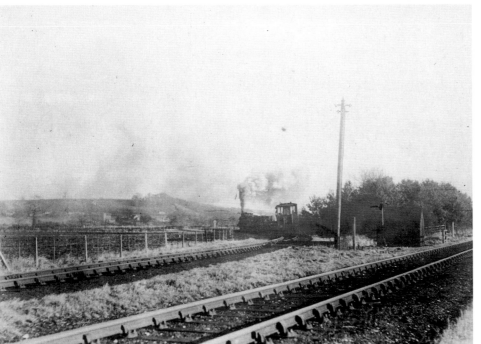

LEFT: *The divergence of the Kirbymoorside and Pickering branch (left) and the Malton line at Cawton. This was 'Gilling Parliamentary Junction' where the Act of Parliament showed the Gilling & Pickering as officially beginning. However, there was no actual junction here as the NER decided to make the junction at the station and the two routes ran as separate single lines until they parted company.* (William Hayes/by courtesy of Raymond H. Hayes)

Scarborough Road Junction, Malton, viewed from the Malton & Driffield line in July 1964. The M&D's route into Malton turns to the left through the bridge, while the Thirsk & Malton heads up the 1 in 55 gradient towards the bridge over the York—Scarborough line. (P. Howat)

Sunbeck signal box, at the apex of the triangular junction off the East Coast Main Line at Pilmoor. The fireman of D49/2 4-4-0 No.62774 The Staintondale has just given up the single line token as his morning Pickering—York train comes off the branch on 15th April 1950. (J.W. Hague/D.V. Beeken Collection)

Helmsley was perhaps the most important place along the Ryedale branch and this turn-of-the-century view shows that its station was furnished with an elegant glass verandah (which survived until the late 1950s). Later photographs show that the signal box was replaced by a taller one with a brick base at the same end-of-platform location.

Ryedale branch rusticity — J39 0-6-0 No.64928 pauses as Pockley Gates for the level crossing to be opened for the branch goods to pass on its way on 26th May 1960. (J.S. Gilks)

NER 0-4-4T No.2088 runs over the crossing into Nawton station where some villagers are dressed up and waiting to join a Pickering—York train to go on their travels. The cottages on the right are for railway employees. The date is between 1910 and 1916. (Raymond H. Hayes)

Kirbymoorside station, before the spelling was altered from 'Kirby-moorside', probably around 1900. The frock-coated gentleman on the right is likely to be Richard Jennings, who was station master until 1901, and the lady next to him is presumably his wife.
(by courtesy of John Bowes/P. Howat collection)

LEFT: *An NER 'BTP' 0-4-4T brings a train from Pickering into Kirbymoorside station, between 1910 and 1914. Viewed from the road bridge a scene of some animation is revealed, with a fair complement of passengers and some barrowloads of baskets and parcels for loading. Another locomotive (a '1001' class 0-6-0) is shunting in the goods yard.*
(William Hayes/by courtesy of Raymond H. Hayes)

RIGHT: *Under a lively sky a D20 4-4-0 heads through Riseborough cutting, beyond Sinnington, with a train for Pickering in June 1938.* (Raymond H. Hayes)

BELOW: *The last ramblers' excursion on the Ryedale branch ran from Bradford on 3rd May 1964, three months before closure. Equipped with boots and rucksacks, the ramblers leave Kirbymoorside station to begin their walks; two conducted rambles (both of sixteen miles and described as "strenuous") had been organised which they had some six hours to complete.*
(T.E. Walker)

ROSEDALE

In the 1850s ironstone deposits were found in the remote hills around Rosedale; when quarrying began, the ironstone was taken by road to Pickering and despatched from there by rail. The chapter on the Esk Valley line records the building of the North Yorkshire & Cleveland Railway from Picton to Stokesley and on to Grosmont. On the same date that this was extended from Ingleby to Kildale, 6th April 1858, the Ingleby Mining Co. opened a mineral railway from Burton Head to what became Ingleby Junction (and later Battersby). With a view to the better opening up of access to the ironstone to be mined in the remote Cleveland Hills, the NYCR (soon to be taken over by the North Eastern Railway) obtained powers in 1858 to purchase this private line and extend it to Rosedale. This eleven-mile route incorporated a self-acting incline, on a 1 in 5 gradient, at Ingleby and was opened on 27th March 1861.

Four years later, when new ironstone deposits began to be worked on the east side of the valley, a branch was opened to East Rosedale on 18th August 1865 from a point on the earlier route known as Blakey Junction. It was as wild and inhospitable an area as any on the NER and offered no prospect of any passenger traffic. Ironstone was the only commodity originating on the Rosedale branch and production fluctuated, reaching a peak of over 560,000 tons in 1873.

For working the Rosedale branch from the mines as far as the Ingleby Incline, a locomotive shed was built at Rosedale. For some years former Stockton & Darlington Railway long-boilered

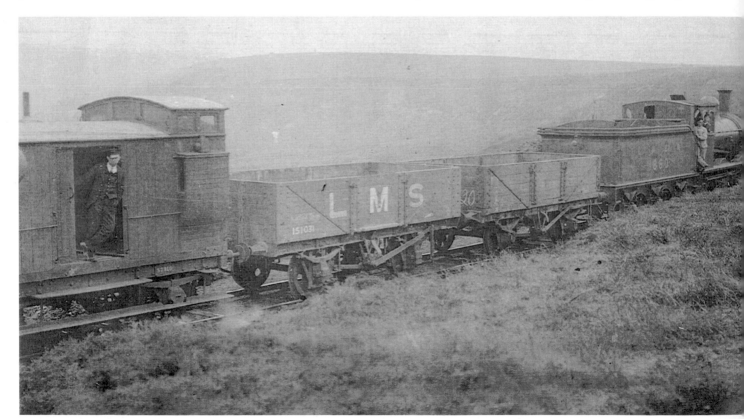

0-6-0s provided the motive power, while latterly three NER Class P (LNER Class J24) 0-6-0s were stationed there. Because of the problems entailed in lowering locomotives down the incline, as much repair work as possible was done at Rosedale. Only if a works overhaul was needed was a locomotive sent down, which involved removing the middle wheels so that the engine could go over the crest of the incline.

Not long after the LNER took over the lines in 1923, the ironstone began to be worked out and production ceased in 1925. However, the railway continued in use for the recovery from huge tips of the calcine dust generated during the 'roasting' process, but once all this had been removed the Rosedale system was closed in 1928. One of the 0-6-0s remained for use on demolition trains and was finally lowered down the incline the following June, bringing the end to a remarkable moorland outpost.

LEFT: *The remoteness of the Rosedale line is evident in this view of J24 No.1860 near Sled Shoe crossing.*
(R.A. Baldwin collection)

BELOW: *The foot of the Ingleby Incline; the minder of the bottom winding house enjoys a smoke on the bench in the spring sunshine.*
(Ken Hoole Study Centre)

The winter wonderland was not quite so much fun on the Rosedale line. S&D 0-6-0 No.1128 and gang battle through the drifts while bowler-hatted managers watch and offer encouragement — but keep their hands warm in their pockets! During the severe winter of 1916/7 the line was completely blocked for a period of five weeks.
(Ken Hoole Study Centre)

Locomotive repairs at Rosedale were not easy at the best of times but the winter weather could make them almost manageable. Stockton & Darlington 0-6-0 No.1126 is under the sheerlegs, wheels removed in Arctic conditions, c1900.
(Ken Hoole Study Centre)

The works at East Rosedale c1920 around the time ironstone mining was coming to an end. However, waste dust, produced in the calcinating kilns, was being reclaimed. This was recovered from the tip on the left of the photograph and taken to Teesside. Regular despatches of calcine dust were made from 1920 until all the tips had been cleared.
(Ken Hoole Study Centre)

J24 0-6-0 No.1860 (with tender cab to protect against the elements) alongside the depots at East Rosedale.
(Ken Hoole Study Centre)

LEFT: *The Rosedale ironstone industry has left plenty of industrial archaeology to explore. The remains of the original kilns at Rosedale West were still to be seen on 5th May 1979.*
(T.J. Edgington)

BELOW *The site of the engine shed at Rosedale West in 1979. After the closure of the railway, the shed was dismantled in 1939 and the stone used to build the village hall at Hutton-le-Hole, a village some five miles away.*
(T.J. Edgington)

THE FORGE VALLEY BRANCH

Along the south eastern fringe of the North York Moors ran a branch line between Pickering and Scarborough. This was the Forge Valley branch, a peaceful and little-known rural backwater which has already been closed for over half a century.

Thoughts of such a line were aired in the Scarborough & Whitby Railway proposals of 1864 as a route from Pickering which would pass through the Forge Valley to join the SWR at Scalby. Nothing materialised of either but when the SWR did finally get under way in 1872 a scheme was put forward for a branch from West Ayton to Scalby. However, in 1873 a separate company — the Forge Valley Railway — presented a Bill for its own route from Ayton and, seeing the prospect of useful feeder traffic, the SWR recommended supporting it.

At this point the powerful North Eastern Railway entered the scene; keen as always to maintain its monopoly, it proposed to construct its own route from Pickering to Scarborough if the Forge Valley Railway promoters withdrew. The NER *did* build the line — eventually — and it opened on 1st May 1882. The 16¼-mile branch took a different course into Scarborough from that in the earlier suggestions as instead of passing through the Forge Valley to Scalby it veered south eastwards to join the York—Scarborough line at Seamer.

Interestingly, the branch as built did not really pass through the Forge Valley at all, even though it possessed a station *named* Forge Valley. Nevertheless it was always known as the Forge Valley branch!

Of the branch's working life there is little to be said as it was wholly unremarkable! A basic timetable of four trains a day either way served the agricultural communities over the years, while a feature of branch operations was the use of Sentinel steam railcars, first introduced on the Forge Valley service in 1928. One of the few incidents of any great note occurred during the Second World War when an escaped barrage balloon became entangled with the telegraph wires!

However, the inevitable downfall of the Forge Valley branch lay in the fact that its stations were some distance from the villages they purported to serve, so that when bus services were developed — passing actually through the villages — they had no difficulty in taking passenger traffic from the trains. Only two years into nationalisation British Railways made the easy economy of discontinuing the service from 5th June 1950 and few probably really missed it. The western extremity between Pickering and Thornton Dale remained open for stone traffic and was not finally closed until 1964.

Ebberston station c1910, with the station master and his young porter together with a lively assortment of village youngsters. Note the NER poster advertising a range of the advantageous tourist tickets which the company provided, along with luggage in advance. As with so many rural stations, the horticulture has been carefully tended and the creeper has become well established in the eighteen years or so since it opened. Ebberston station was renamed from Wilton in 1903, but it wasn't really near either; the nearest village was Allerston! (J.R. Lidster collection)

Snainton was the busiest station on the branch and the only one with a passing loop. Signals and points were controlled from the lever shed by the telegraph pole on the left-hand platform. An unusual feature of the station was a hippopotamus skull mounted on a bracket under the platform canopy! (A. Pickup/J.R. Lidster collection)

Sawdon station c1926, but still with NER notice boards. During World War II the station became unusually busy when its loading dock was used for armoured vehicles for the Army which had taken over Wydale and Brompton Halls. (J.R. Lidster collection)

Forge Valley station c1904. It was not actually in the valley which gave the branch its name, but in West Ayton. (Peter Smith/J.R. Lidster collection)

During the late 1920s and early 1930s the LNER purchased from Sentinel-Cammell a fleet of steam railcars to provide a more economical way of operating its local services. British Queen, one of the 100hp six-cylinder cars built in 1929, was regularly used on the Forge Valley service and is seen at Seamer Junction in December 1939 bound for Pickering.
(Neville Pick/J.R. Lidster collection)

FROM SCARBOROUGH TO WHITBY

Running along the coast between Scarborough and Whitby was one of England's most scenic branch lines. The connection of these two towns and ports seems a logical one but it proved difficult to achieve and was, in fact, the last link in the railway network of the North York Moors area.

The Scarborough & Whitby Railway Co. was formed in 1871 to construct a line between the two places but although construction began in 1872 it was to take thirteen years to complete it. Financial problems and the difficult nature of the terrain made it a protracted affair. Tunnels were required at Scarborough and Ravenscar, but the greatest engineering challenge was presented by the need to cross the River Esk at Whitby by a massive brick viaduct 915ft in length and 120ft high. Lack of funds held up progress and twice, in 1878 and 1879, the directors met to consider winding up the company.

However, the line was eventually opened on 16th July 1885. From the outset the line was worked by the North Eastern Railway and was formally absorbed by that company in 1898.

The Scarborough—Whitby line was always a difficult one to work. For a start, the junction at Scarborough was a trailing one outside the station, so a reversal was required almost immediately. Then there were its fearsome gradients — the climb to the summit on the cliffs at Ravenscar was at 1 in 41 from the south and 1 in 39 from the north, while another 1 in 43 climb took trains back up to the cliffs from Robin Hood's Bay. At Prospect Hill Junction, Whitby, the line joined the Whitby, Redcar & Middlesbrough Union Railway's route northwards via Staithes which had climbed from its junction with the Pickering line on the banks of the Esk to Whitby West Cliff station. Another reversal was needed there for trains to reach the main station at Whitby Town.

The NER soon sought to capitalise on the line's scenic attractions, proclaiming it to be "21 miles of the most picturesque railway in the British Isles". Both it and the LNER offered a wide variety of 'runabout' tickets covering lines in the Scarborough and Whitby areas, while the LNER's popular scenic excursions from the West Riding and Hull took in the coast line on either the outward or return journey.

Holiday traffic was at its height in the pre-war and immediate post-war years and such was the occupancy of the single line sections that the local goods had to run in the evening when the line was quieter. In winter, however, things were considerably less busy when three or four trains a day would suffice.

Major changes came in May 1958 when the Staithes line closed, resulting in trains running through between Scarborough and Middlesbrough being re routed via Grosmont and the Esk Valley (with yet another reversal at Battersby!). At the same time diesel multiple units took over passenger services, greatly simplifying the reversals, while the improved views obtainable from their large windows were appreciated by passengers.

Unfortunately the good times were coming to an end. As related in previous chapters, the 'Beeching Plan' portended the closure of all Whitby's railways, including the Scarborough line. The closure was bitterly contested but the contrast of a few busy summer months with empty seats the rest of the year produced the inevitable result and the last train ran on Saturday 6th March 1965.

Even then the line refused to lie still. A preservation scheme came and went in 1966, then in 1967 five local authorities combined to investigate the possibility of having the line re-opened through a subsidy from the rates but eventually quaked at an estimated annual loss of £23,000. That was the end of revival hopes and in 1968 tracklifting began. The section between Hawsker and Whitby remained *in situ* for several more years in connection with the possible mining of potash in the area but was finally recovered in 1974. In 1975 most of the trackbed was acquired by Scarborough Borough Council for use as a footpath; a splendid coastal walk can now be enjoyed — as can refreshments in the tea rooms occupying the station offices and gardens at Cloughton!

A Scarborough—Whitby DMU calls at Ravenscar, summit of the line close to some of Yorkshire's highest cliffs, on 2nd May 1964. The buildings in the background are among the few achievements of a Victorian plan to develop Ravenscar as an invigorating resort. (J.S Gilks)

During the mid-1950s various LMS-designed classes appeared on the coast line, most notably Fairburn Class 4 2-6-4Ts. No.42084 heaves a Scarborough-bound train over the summit of the climb into Ravenscar station on 23rd July 1957. On the left of the picture the gradient board indicates the end of the 1 in 39 ascent and the start of a more modest 1 in 1,571 descent through the station, though that soon steepened to 1 in 41; the change of gradient is noticeable at the second coach of the train. (Ken Hoole)

Summers on the Scarborough—Whitby line were marked by scenic excursions to Whitby from the West Riding, begun by the LNER in the 1930s. This one, taken on the cliffs above Robin Hood's Bay on the 1 in 39 climb to Ravenscar on 26th June 1955, is double-headed by North Eastern Railway G5 0-4-4T No.67289 and LNER B1 4-6-0 No.61216. The train will have travelled out via Pickering and Grosmont, before returning via the coast line — a superb itinerary. (Ken Hoole)

B1 4-6-0 No.61037 blasts up the 1 in 39 to Ravenscar with a Stockton—Scarborough train on 11th August 1957. The train is passing the chimney of the disused Whitaker's brickworks which was opened in an old alum quarry. A siding connection was provided and the shunting arrangements were strict to ensure that wagons were not left standing on the gradient. The chimney was demolished in April 1963. (Ken Hoole)

Heading north from Scarborough, Cloughton was the first station with a passing loop and also had the only manned level crossing on the line. Platform-mounted signal boxes were a feature of stations on the branch. This view, looking north, was taken on 4th March 1965, two days before the last trains ran. However, the station buildings survive as a guest house and tea rooms, with the trackbed incorporated into the gardens. (J.S Gilks)

Seven miles north of Scarborough was the single platform of Hayburn Wyke, seen here on a warm July day in 1964. The station served an attractive cove popular with trippers and a hotel; even though there was little in the way of local population it used to have a station master whose residence is beyond the far end of the platform. The station became an unstaffed halt in 1955 and the platform building was converted for use as a camping cottage. The gardens were maintained by the Stainton Dale station master under whose control it thereafter came. (David Sutcliffe)

Raising the echoes at the site of the old brickworks north of Ravenscar are Class A8 4-6-2T No.69865 (rebuilt from an NER 4-4-4T in 1935) and B1 4-6-0 No.61115 with a scenic excursion on 26th June 1955. Although the climb to the summit was nominally a consistent 1 in 39, there was in fact an easing of the gradient at this point, discernible after the second carriage. Five coaches were the maximum for one locomotive or eight coaches for double heading. More could often have been handled under good conditions but those did not always prevail; sea frets, for instance, could leave rails greasy and make working the line particularly difficult. (Ken Hoole)

North Eastern Railway Class D 4-4-4T No.2151 at Robin Hood's Bay heading a Scarborough—Saltburn train in August 1922. In the 1930s the LNER decided that these engines would be of even more use on the steeply-graded lines of north Yorkshire if rebuilt as 4-6-2 tanks. All were converted to this form between 1931 and 1936 and as LNER Class A8 became even more closely associated with the coast line until diesel units took over in 1958. (T. Horn/Ken Hoole collection)

A bust moment captured at Robin Hood's Bay c1904/5 as an NER '1001' class 0-6-0 on the local goods passes a Scarborough-bound train. This was the most important and busiest station on the line — serving the picturesque fishing village which has long attracted visitors and holidaymakers — and watering facilities for locomotives were provided at the ends of both platforms. (T.J. Edgington collection)

The Scarborough—Whitby line was at its most scenic on the cliff-top stretches above the North Sea. Easing down the 1 in 39 descent from Ravenscar in July 1964, this Whitby-bound DMU affords its passengers a magnificent view of the wide sweep of Robin Hood's Bay with the fishing village of that name nestling in the cliffs in the distance. (David Sutcliffe)

A Scarborough—Middlesbrough DMU calls at Robin Hood's Bay on a snowy day in January 1964, a local lady just having alighted after a shopping trip to Scarborough. After descending from Ravenscar, the train would begin climbing again at the end of the platform at 1 in 43 towards the cliffs above Whitby. (David Sutcliffe)

ABOVE: *The thirteen arches of Larpool Viaduct — here being crossed by a BR Class 3 2-6-0 on a Darlington to Scarborough train — carry the railway over the River Esk at Whitby. On the far bank of the river is the Whitby & Pickering line, while at a higher level is the WRMU line climbing towards Whitby West Cliff.* (Ken Hoole)

RIGHT: *The imposing presence of Larpool Viaduct at Whitby is still a dominating feature in the landscape despite over 35 years of disuse. The viaduct has a maximum height of 125ft and contains around five million bricks. The three piers in the river are skewed so as not to deflect the course of the water.*

LEFT: *A Scarborough to Darlington DMU descends from Prospect Hill to Whitby Town on 21st May 1960; it is about to pass under the Larpool Viaduct which it will just have crossed on its way from Scarborough.* (J.S Gilks)

ABOVE: *On a spring afternoon in May 1958, BR 2-6-4T No.80118 passes under Larpool Viaduct (carrying the Scarborough line) running out of Whitby along the bank of the River Esk with the 4.05pm to Battersby.* (C. Hogg/Colour-Rail BRE1236)

RIGHT: *A memorable last day special was run over th Scarborough—Whitby and Grosmont—Malton lines on 6t March 1965, double-headed by preserved LNER K4 2-6- No.3442 The Great Marquess and K1 2-6-0 No.62005. Th 'Whitby Moors Rail Tour', which had started a Manchester, is approaching Stainton Dale.* (David Sutcliffe

The unusual signal box at Prospect Hill Junction, Whitby, on 24th May 1960, straddling the line up from Whitby Town. The photograph is taken from a diesel multiple unit which has come up from Whitby Town and, after reversing, is heading off towards Scarborough. (J.S Gilks)

Whitby West Cliff station looking north on 22nd May 1960. Following closure of the Loftus line the track has been truncated beyond the bridge, but trains to and from Scarborough continued to reverse here. However, it was not well placed for visitors to Whitby 'proper' and it closed a year later on 12th June 1961. (J.S Gilks)

Two dramatic coastal routes ran north and south of Whitby, formed as completely separate companies. The Whitby, Redcar & Middlesbrough Union Railway was formed in 1866 to construct a line from Ruswarp (on the Whitby & Pickering line) to Loftus where it would meet the existing former Cleveland Railway route. Work was not begun until 1871 due to lack of funds but there then followed trouble with the contractor who was eventually dispensed with in 1873. Meanwhile the company decided to start its railway from Whitby (at Bog Hall Junction) and pursue a more coastal course to Sandsend than that originally envisaged.

Continuing financial problems meant that the WRMUR was unable to finish the project and in 1875 the North Eastern Railway agreed to take it over and complete it. In fact, it had to create another new route further inland between Sandsend and Kettleness to bypass a poorly-constructed stretch which had collapsed into the sea. At last the line was opened on 3rd December 1883 and six years later the NER, which had been leasing and working it, formally absorbed the WRMUR.

The first train services ran between Whitby and Saltburn, but two years later the coast route from Scarborough was opened, meeting the Loftus line at Prospect Hill Junction, and a Scarborough—Saltburn service was then instituted. On the opening of the Loftus line a station had been opened at Whitby West Cliff and served these through trains; however, if a train from Scarborough was to call at Whitby Town a reversal at West Cliff was necessary. In 1933 the LNER altered the pattern of train services to now run between Scarborough, Whitby and Middlesbrough and this inspired a considerable growth in passenger traffic during the summer months. A shuttle service between Whitby Town and West Cliff obviated the necessity for through trains to make time-consuming reversals.

What a scenic line this was! From an elevated position at Whitby West Cliff, it dropped at 1 in 60 to an almost beachside position at Sandsend, then climbed at 1 in 62 and 1 in 57 back up to the cliffs. Curves and gradients abounded, as well as a series of five iron and steel viaducts taking the railway across inlets in the cliffs. Four of them came in little over a mile — Sandsend, East Row, Newholm Beck and Upgang. However, the longest (700ft) and highest (152ft) was at Staithes and so exposed was its position that it was fitted with a wind gauge which caused a bell to ring if the wind was too strong for trains to cross the viaduct safely.

During the mid-1950s traffic began to decline as road transport grew in popularity. With Sandsend Tunnel needing repairs and the continuing costs of maintaining the viaducts, British Railways took the decision to close the line and the last trains between Whitby and Loftus ran on 3rd May 1958. Over the next couple of years the viaducts were dismantled, an ignominious end to a railway built at considerable expense and with such high (but mostly unfulfilled) expectations.

An alternative route for Whitby—Middlesbrough trains already existed via the Esk Valley and Battersby, but the closure of Whitby's northern coastal line was a portent of things to come. The Beeching Report was still five years away, but within seven years two more of Whitby's scenic railways would have been erased from the map.

A notable feature of the Whitby, Redcar & Middlesbrough Union line was the number of iron and steel viaducts which carried it across inlets along the coast. LNER L1 2-6-4T No.67754 crosses East Row Viaduct, Sandsend, in 1954. (Colour-Rail BRE737)

On 3rd May 1958 the 4.20pm Middlesbrough—Scarborough formed the last train over the Loftus—Staithes—Whitby route and this view from the train shows it crossing the East Row Viaduct at Sandsend, watched by a lone girl on the shingle. The line had dropped to almost sea level but soon climbed again at 1 in 60 to gain an elevated position on the approach to Whitby. (Ian L. Wright)

The last rites on the Whitby—Loftus route were performed on 3rd May 1958. A headboard sums up the feelings surrounding the closure as BR 2-6-4T No.80116 stands at Whitby West Cliff after bringing in the last train, the 4.20pm from Middlesbrough to Scarborough. West Cliff remained open for Scarborough—Whitby trains to reverse there until 12th June 1961.

ABOVE: *The WRMU line joined the Whitby & Pickering at Bog Hall Junction. LMS Fairburn 2-6-4T No.42084 brings a train from Scarborough down the 1 in 50 gradient on 21st June 1957.* (Ken Hoole)

SANDSEND FROM THE SOUTH

G 5379

RIGHT: *Sandsend Viaduct awaits its fate on 22nd May 1960. Two years have elapsed since the last trains crossed it, the rails have been lifted and soon the demolition men will move in.* (J.S. Gilks)

LEFT: *A fine view of Sandsend showing the proximity of the railway to the sea at this point. In this mid-1930s view, notable for its almost total lack of road traffic, the goods shed at East Row can be seen beyond which are three six-wheel camping coaches. The railway then crosses East Row Viaduct to Sandsend station behind which three more such vehicles can just be discerned.* (David Sutcliffe collection)

The LNER introduced the idea of camping coaches in 1933 and sites which could hardly fail to be popular were the two at Sandsend. In 1934 a party of spirited young ladies was occupying this former GNR six-wheeler at the station site directly above the seashore and had put one of their ladders up to the roof. There, with deckchairs and gramophone, they enjoy a spot of sunbathing where they can watch the gentle waves breaking on the beach. There would be a health and safety rule against this today.....(NRM 72/94)

As the North Sea laps restlessly on the beach, A8 4-6-2T No.9881 runs along the cliffs above Sandsend with a train which includes a fitted van in 1948. Nationalisation has come but nothing much has changed yet. (Ken Hoole Study Centre)

To many train-struck youngsters the idea of a holiday in a railway carriage next to passing trains must have seemed a dream come true. And for those not seized by the railway bug, a camping coach holiday must also have been fun in the attractive settings chosen for the sites. This is East Row, Sandsend, in the early 1950s with campers enjoying the sunshine (though perhaps not Teddy, ignominiously left face down on the ground — shame!). Three coaches were located at Sandsend station, with another three in the sidings at East Row. (BR)

A8 No.9858 runs along the clifftops near Kettleness carrying express headlamps as it heads towards Whitby during the summer of 1947. The first two vehicles are NER clerestory coaches of some vintage.
(Ken Hoole Study Centre)

The biggest of the route's viaducts was at Staithes, with seventeen spans in a length of 233 yards and a maximum height of 152ft. Construction had been started by the Whitby, Redcar & Middlesbrough Union Railway but after the NER took over in 1875 it had the viaduct strengthened with cross-bracing before it was opened to traffic. The viaduct was dismantled in 1960.
(David Sutcliffe collection)

ESK VALLEY BRANCH

The line carrying trains today from Middlesbrough to Whitby travel over what is known as the Esk Valley branch but its origins are more intricate. The section between Grosmont and Whitby, for instance, forms part of the historic Whitby & Pickering Railway.

In 1854 the North Yorkshire & Cleveland Railway was formed to build a line from Picton (on the Leeds Northern route between Northallerton and Eaglescliffe) to Grosmont, with a view to exploiting ironstone deposits in the area. It was opened between Picton and Stokesley on 2nd March 1857, on to Ingleby on 1st February 1858 and to Kildale on 6th April 1858. The NYCR was taken over by the North Eastern Railway in 1859 and it was that company which opened the route through to Grosmont on 2nd October 1865. This enabled a through service between Whitby and Stockton to be operated.

A station known as Ingleby Junction was established in 1868 on the opening of a branch to Nunthorpe on the Middlesbrough & Guisborough line. The station's name was changed to Battersby Junction ten years later and to plain Battersby in 1893.

The iron industry was short-lived; Glaisdale, for instance, had an ironworks with three blast furnaces but this was defunct by 1876. The branch thereafter served a number of isolated communities along the Esk Valley and might well have been expected to perish with so many others in the cuts of the 1960s.

The line from Battersby to Picton was closed on 14th June 1954 and this made Battersby a 'terminus' as Whitby trains now reversed there in order to use the Nunthorpe branch. When in 1958 the coast line north of Whitby was abandoned, the Middlesbrough trains were re-routed via Grosmont and Battersby, a move which was ultimately the Esk Valley's salvation.

The 'Beeching Report' advocated the withdrawal of all Whitby's passenger trains but the ensuing furore resulted in the reprieve of the Middlesbrough service, doubtless in recognition of the hardship which would have been caused to the Esk Valley villages, possibly also as a 'sop' to Whitby which feared for its commercial future if left with no rail connection.

And so the Esk Valley branch clings on, though only just. The line is operated on a very minimalist basis with all stations, including Whitby, reduced to unstaffed status. Four-wheeled 'Pacer' trains bounce along the branch on just a handful of trains per day, a far cry from more prosperous times. A taste of better things came about in the last year or so, however, in the shape of occasional steam-hauled trains working through to Whitby from the North Yorkshire Moors Railway, though in September 2000 a ban on steam locomotives was imposed due to two weak bridges. Circumstances like this are indicative of the tenuous grip which financially-straitened branches like the Esk Valley maintain on existence, but one can hope for the necessary investment to enable the Esk Valley branch to face a more certain future.

A G5 0-4-4T crosses the Esk at Glaisdale during the 1950s. On 23rd July 1930 flooding following a torrential storm washed away the original stone bridge; the bridge was rebuilt and the line re-opened on 25th May 1931, but less than four months later the same thing happened again! The bridge was again rebuilt, this time as a girder structure, and the line restored to use on 29th August 1932. (J.W. Armstrong Trust)

Whitby's remaining railway has declined in status in recent years, its train service, general facilities and maintenance being best described as 'minimal'. The four-wheel 'Pacer' units were all that was offered for the Whitby—Middlesbrough service, typified by this working at Glaisdale on 5th October 1996. With the station unstaffed and the buildings sold into private ownership, a 'bus shelter' has been thoughtfully provided. Conventional signalling was abolished and 'no signalman' key token working introduced in 1989, with Glaisdale the only passing place between Whitby and Battersby. (T.J. Edgington)

Lealholm looking towards Whitby, was another rural Esk Valley station not lacking in facilities which include signal box, goods shed and coal drops — though, again, just a single platform. This view was taken in NER days c1905. (NRM 472/86)

The neat and tidy station at Castleton in the early years of the twentieth century. Crossing facilities were provided but only one platform, so two passenger trains could not pass there. The substantial signal box is well adorned with enamel advertising notices: Venus Soap (advertised twice!) reminds us that as it "saves rubbing", home laundry was a laborious manual process in those days, while Willows, Holt and Willows' linseed and cotton cakes would be of interest to the local farming community. In 1965 BR renamed the station Castleton Moor, presumably to avoid confusion with the Castleton near Rochdale. (NRM 335/86)

Castleton (back from Castleton Moor) on Sunday 2nd September 1981, with a Whitby-bound DMU arriving and the signalman ready to exchange single line tokens. This view differs from the one of some 80 years earlier in that it has gained a platform on the up loop and the brick signal box on the down platform has been replaced by one on the opposite side. The oil lamps have also yielded to modern electric lights. Sunday services only ran during summer months and this was probably the last Sunday of that year's timetable. (Gavin Morrison)

Battersby station in the early 1950s, looking towards Whitby and Middlesbrough. It possessed two lengthy platforms with the line continuing behind the photographer to Picton, while at the far end of the left-hand platform is a bay platform with its own run-round loop. Beyond the station the line divides to Middlesbrough via Nunthorpe and to Whitby via the Esk Valley. Watering facilities were provided at both ends of the station; note the crane on the up platform extending over the track with a pulley and chain to lower the leather 'bag'. Battersby ceased to be a through station in 1954 when the line from there to Picton closed. The up platform then became redundant and the footbridge was removed, though the track was kept to enable locomotives to run round.

RIGHT: *Battersby station on 3rd May 1958. A8 4-6-2T No.69877 is on a Middlesbrough—Whitby train and is ready to take the Esk Valley branch, while on the right a train is heading via Nunthorpe to Middlesbrough. Both will have reversed in the station.* (Ian L. Wright)

Harsh conditions on the Esk Valley line in February 1902 — NER 0-6-0 No.659 finds itself embattled in a snowdrift at Battersby.
(J.R. Lidster collection)